PHILADELI

THE CITY AT A GLAN(

Wachovia Building
This 1928 H-shaped high-rise,
architects Simon & Simon, feat
by the Piccirilli Brothers. It wa
by local firm Cope Linder in 1996.
123-151 S Broad Street

Wanamaker Building
The city's pioneer department store,
Wanamaker's, may be long gone, but Daniel
Burnham's palatial granite building, opened
in 1910, is a reminder of its golden age.
1300 Market Street

One Liberty Place
The stepped spire of Helmut Jahn's Chrysler-
esque skyscraper, completed in 1987, singles
it out on the skyline. Two Liberty Place next
door was also designed by Jahn.
1650 Market Street

City Hall
This massive structure, which took 30 years
to build, is the geographic and ceremonial
centre of Philadelphia, crowned by a statue
of its founder, William Penn. Take the lift
to the top for a stunning panoramic view.
See p013

Comcast Center
The tallest in the city, Robert AM Stern's
skyscraper is an understated sliver of glass.
See p012

Inquirer Building
Rankin, Kellogg and Crane's iconic Beaux Arts
building has housed *The Philadelphia Inquirer*
newspaper since 1925. It's a counterpoint
to City Hall, located six blocks to the south.
400-440 N Broad Street

INTRODUCTION

THE CHANGING FACE OF THE URBAN SCENE

Philadelphia has, at various points in its history, been one of the world's great cities – the centre of cultural and political activity in colonial America; the first capital of the United States; and the young nation's first industrial giant. But it is just 130km south-west of New York, and in the national perception the city often seems to take a back seat to the Big Apple. In 2005, *The New York Times* called it 'the next borough', a nickname that outraged many locals. And with good reason. Philadelphia is a sophisticated, energetic city that is once again coming into its own, thanks largely to a young, diverse population keen on carving out a metropolis that is eminently liveable and refreshingly unpretentious.

That said, you won't get a taste of the best parts of Philly if you stay on the tourist track. Instead, explore its neighbourhoods. Whether historic (Old City) or emerging (Northern Liberties), they're all distinctive and easily accessible, and peppered with many excellent restaurants and one-off shops. And Philadelphians are friendly, savvy urbanites. Their quirky, self-effacing attitude is part of what makes this city so alluring.

Between its urban and architectural attractions, the charm of the surrounding Pennsylvania countryside and long list of escape destinations, you certainly won't be stuck for things to do here or be hankering to hotfoot it to NYC. But don't try to fit everything in. Philly, take our word for it, is a city that you'll want to revisit.

ESSENTIAL INFO

FACTS, FIGURES AND USEFUL ADDRESSES

TOURIST OFFICE
Independence Visitor Center
6th Street/Market Street
T 215 965 7676
independencevisitorcenter.com

TRANSPORT
Car hire
Avis
Philadelphia International Airport
T 215 492 0900
Public transport
T 215 580 7800
septa.com
Subway runs daily, 5am to midnight. Night Owl buses operate in-between. The daytime Phlash bus stops at 25 key locations
Taxis
PHL Taxi
T 215 232 2000
Cabs can also be hailed in the street

EMERGENCY SERVICES
Emergencies
T 911
24-hour pharmacy
CVS
1826 Chestnut Street
T 215 972 0909
cvs.com

CONSULATE
British Honorary Consulate
33rd floor, 1818 Market Street
T 215 557 7665
ukinusa.fco.gov.uk

MONEY
American Express
Suite H, 1600 John F Kennedy Boulevard
T 215 587 2300
travel.americanexpress.com

POSTAL SERVICES
Post office
3000 Chestnut Street
T 1 800 275 8777
www.usps.com
Shipping
UPS
1229 Chestnut Street
T 215 568 4555

BOOKS
Louis I Kahn by Robert McCarter (Phaidon Press)
Philadelphia Architecture: A Guide to the City by John Andrew Gallery (Paul Dry Books)
Philly Fiction (Don Ron Books)
Still Philadelphia: A Photographic History 1890-1940 by Fredric Miller (Temple University Press)

WEBSITES
Architecture
philadelphiacfa.org
Arts
icaphila.org
Newspapers
philadelphiaweekly.com
philly.com

COST OF LIVING
Taxi from Philadelphia International Airport to city centre
$25
Cappuccino
$3.50
Packet of cigarettes
$6
Daily newspaper
$0.75
Bottle of champagne
$90

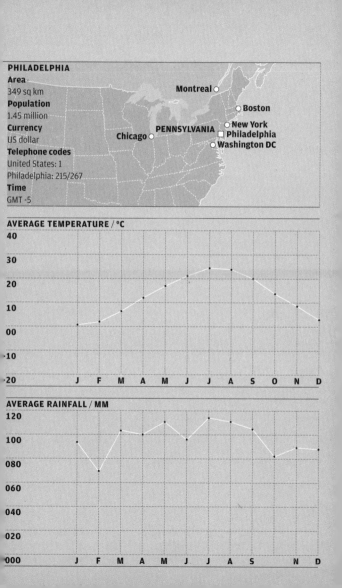

PHILADELPHIA

Area
349 sq km

Population
1.45 million

Currency
US dollar

Telephone codes
United States: 1
Philadelphia: 215/267

Time
GMT -5

Montreal
Boston
New York
PENNSYLVANIA
Chicago
Philadelphia
Washington DC

AVERAGE TEMPERATURE / °C

40
30
20
10
00
-10
-20

J F M A M J J A S O N D

AVERAGE RAINFALL / MM

120
100
080
060
040
020
000

J F M A M J J A S O N D

NEIGHBOURHOODS
THE AREAS YOU NEED TO KNOW AND WHY

To help you navigate the city, we've chosen the most interesting districts (see below and the map inside the back cover) and colour-coded our featured venues, according to their location; those venues that are outside these areas are not coloured.

UNIVERSITY CITY
Six colleges and universities are located here so, as you'd expect, this is an area with a lively going-out and arts culture. Don't miss the White Dog Cafe (see p037), the ICA (see p028) and The Rotunda (4014 Walnut Street, T 215 573 3234), one of the city's edgier performance venues.

SOUTH PHILADELPHIA
South Philly is largely residential, though it gets attention for South Street's nightlife, Fabric Row on S 4th Street and the Italian Market – Isgro Pasticceria (1009 Christian Street, T 215 923 3092), in particular, is known for its baked goods. You'll also find myriad Asian and Latino businesses.

FAIRMOUNT/ART MUSEUM
Most people know this neighbourhood for the Philadelphia Museum of Art (see p014) and Fairmount Park, which begins here. The district's quiet streets are a draw too, as are tours of the massive 1829 Eastern State Penitentiary (2124 Fairmount Avenue, T 215 236 3300). To the west, Kelly Drive offers spectacular river and city views.

WASHINGTON SQUARE WEST
The area between Society Hill and tony Rittenhouse Square languished for years as urban renewal swirled around it. Gentrification here is catching up, but for now the area still mixes hipness and grit. Check out its restaurants and bars, such as Mercato (see p030) and APO (see p031).

OLD CITY
The oldest part of Philadelphia, along the Delaware waterfront, has been reborn as a district of lofts, smart shops and restaurants at its northern end, while there are stately row houses in Society Hill to the south. Independence Mall gets choked with tourists but quiet corners do exist.

CENTER CITY NORTH
Business is the focus of the area north of Market Street. But there is fun to be had; seek out Reading Terminal Market (51 N 12th Street, T 215 922 2317) for local produce and Amish specialities, the PSFS Building (see p066) and the Pennsylvania Academy of the Fine Arts (see p056).

RITTENHOUSE SQUARE
Once the enclave of Philadelphia's élite, this area remains one of the best bets for shopping and dining, especially on Walnut Street. There are office towers to the north and the east, but the south is still lined with attractive low-level streets. Pub & Kitchen (see p044), one of our favourite Philly eateries, is here.

NORTHERN LIBERTIES
Located just outside Philadelphia's original boundaries, this area got its name because William Penn gave everyone who bought land in the city a free plot here. Today, an influx of young residents, who hang out at venues such as North Bowl (see p094), are filling up its row houses and factories.

LANDMARKS
THE SHAPE OF THE CITY SKYLINE

When William Penn founded Philadelphia, he envisioned a city of townhouses ringed by large country estates. The colonists who developed it had other ideas. Dividing and subdividing Penn's lots, they formed a dense urban zone that eventually spilled out miles across the Delaware valley. Modern Philly's sprawl of suburbs, malls and freeways may seem as inscrutable as any metropolitan jumble, but at its core it's a superb piece of urban planning.

Credit for the layout of the area called Center City must go to Penn. His 1682 grid plan – the first of its kind in the US – stands today. Its focal point, literally and symbolically, is City Hall (see p013), whose clock tower defined the skyline for decades, though it has since been eclipsed by an array of skyscrapers, including the Comcast Center (see p012). To the east, heading towards the Delaware River, Philadelphia's colonial beginnings can be seen in Old City, which is anchored by Independence Hall (overleaf).

Today, Philly is not only building upwards, but also dealing with past missteps on the ground, like the no-man's-land along the Delaware waterfront. Created when the Interstate 95 cut through in the 1960s, it's now being reborn as a series of parks and mixed-use projects. Hopefully, future development will maintain the juxtapositions of style and scale that give the Philly cityscape its unique appeal: by turns gritty and polished but always interesting. *For full addresses, see Resources.*

Independence Hall

It's on every tourist's hit list, but the elegance of the building where America declared its independence in 1776 raises it above the sea of bumbags and Bermuda shorts. English-trained master builder Edmund Woolley began designing what was originally the meeting house for Pennsylvania's colonial legislature in 1732, turning to the English country house for inspiration. The result is one of the finest Georgian buildings in the US, topped by the clock tower where the famously cracked Liberty Bell once hung (this is now across the street in the Liberty Bell Center, T 215 965 2305). Restorations have returned Independence Hall to its 18th-century appearance, inside and out. The Long Gallery runs the length of the upper storey and was once the largest public room in the state.

500 Chestnut Street, T 1 800 537 7676, nps.gov/inde

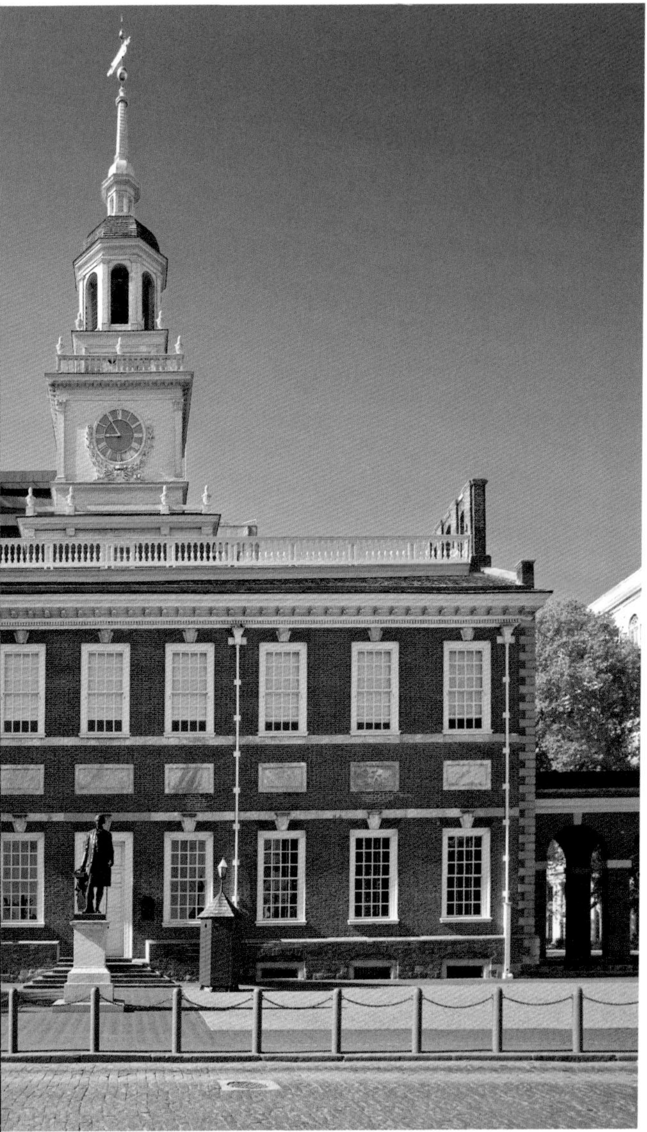

Comcast Center

Standing below this dazzling structure, you feel every bit of its imposing 297m height. And yet the HQ of America's largest cable company, designed by New York-based architects Robert AM Stern, is so reflective, its tapered form so simple, that it slips very quietly into the skyline. That's due in part to the sheer glass skin (the original plan was for a Kasota stone facing) and to the pleated corners and transparent crown. Stern's design, whose eco features make this one of the tallest green buildings in the US, really excels at street level, where an expansive public plaza leads to a 33.5m-high lobby with a winter garden and a 185 sq m HD video screen, The Comcast Experience, designed by NYC's Niles Creative Group.
1701 John F Kennedy Boulevard,
T 215 981 8450

City Hall

When the ground was broken for Philadelphia's City Hall in 1871, architects John McArthur Jr and Thomas U Walter intended it to be the world's tallest structure. By the time construction ended in 1901, the 167m tower had been eclipsed in height, and their fussy Second Empire style was completely outdated. Fortunately, this handsome building has survived various redevelopment schemes and remains an arresting and much-loved symbol of proud, Victorian Philadelphia. Don't miss the 250 or so sculptures carved by Alexander Milne Calder for the interior and exterior, especially the 11.3m-high statue of William Penn that tops them all. You can't just wander into the building, but guided tours and access to the observation deck are run on weekdays.
1 Penn Square, T 215 686 2840

Philadelphia Museum of Art

Probably best known for its front steps,
which appeared in the *Rocky* films,
the 1928 Museum of Art bookmarks the
northern end of the Benjamin Franklin
Parkway. Architects Horace Trumbauer,
with Zantzinger, Borie and Medary
wrapped the building – their museum
as temple – in Minnesota limestone,
limiting the exterior ornamentation
to the bronze griffins on the roofline
and Carl Paul Jennewein's polychrome
figures in the tympanum of the north wing.
Inside is a vast collection of global art
and artefacts, so we suggest concentrating
on the American section. Subterranean
galleries, designed by Frank Gehry, are the
next phase in a 10-year expansion plan that
includes the Perelman Building (see p070).
2600 Benjamin Franklin Parkway,
T 215 763 8100, philamuseum.org

HOTELS

WHERE TO STAY AND WHICH ROOMS TO BOOK

Philly's hotels have long been geared towards the business crowd. Lucrative as that may have been, it's left the city with a glut of bland chains and unremarkable budget options, with not much in-between, except for the odd chintzy B&B. But things are changing.

Center City is the heart of hotel land and the best place to stay to see the main attractions at the closest range. Fans of modernism should check into Loews (see p022), which occupies a landmark tower with commanding views, while the stylish AKA Rittenhouse Square (see p021) offers an unbeatable location and suites large enough to host your entourage. Three well-established but more traditional options are the Four Seasons (1 Logan Square, T 215 963 1500), The Ritz-Carlton (opposite), housed in an early 20th-century bank building, and the elegant Rittenhouse (see p020).

The growing appeal of Philadelphia as a destination in its own right, as opposed to a quick day trip from New York, is evident in the new properties gradually making an entrance in the centre of town. Though several projects have been put on hold, the Kimpton group has made its local debut with Hotel Palomar (overleaf), with interiors by the LA-based Dayna Lee, while Le Méridien (1421 Arch Street, T 215 422 8200) was designed by Philly firm Blackney Hayes Architects. Meanwhile, the Hilton group has announced plans to open a Waldorf-Astoria close to The Ritz-Carlton in Center City. *For full addresses and room rates, see Resources.*

The Ritz-Carlton

The local outpost of The Ritz-Carlton chain, opened in 2000, is located in the Avenue of the Arts area, the stretch of S Broad Street lined with the city's major performance venues. The hotel wins points too for its setting in the 1908 Girard Trust Company Building, designed by McKim, Mead & White. The lobby (above) and 10 Arts restaurant, headed by Eric Ripert of Le Bernardin in New York, take full advantage of the lofty neoclassical space; at night, the acres of white marble are accented by a striking red lighting scheme. The rooms are on the small side and the décor doesn't keep pace with many Ritz properties, but the views of City Hall (see p013) in those facing north are great; book a Superior Room or a suite if you want more space. *10 S Broad Street, T 215 523 8000, ritzcarlton.com/philadelphia*

Hotel Palomar

Set in a restored 1929 high-rise off Rittenhouse Square, the Palomar injects a much-needed dose of contemporary design into the Philly hotel scene. Deco-inspired touches include the recycled-glass fireplace in the lobby and angular lamps and headboards in the 230 rooms and suites (King Deluxe Room, pictured). *117 S 17th Street, T 215 563 5006, hotelpalomar-philadelphia.com*

The Rittenhouse

Visiting VIPs favour The Rittenhouse, a hotel whose grande dame reputation belies the fact it opened as recently as 1989. Local interior designer Marguerite Rodgers did out the 98 rooms and suites in warm neutrals, with patterned fabrics and mahogany furniture, and though very nicely presented, the interiors are a little dated. Even so, it's hard to complain too much given the size of the rooms (at up to 93 sq m, the suites are some of the largest in town), and the views from around half of them are over Rittenhouse Square. Take advantage of the indoor pool, the Adolf Biecker Spa and Salon (T 215 735 6404) and the Lacroix at The Rittenhouse restaurant (T 215 790 2533), which ranks among the city's best eateries.
210 W Rittenhouse Square,
T 215 546 9000, rittenhousehotel.com

AKA Rittenhouse Square

The understated entrance, neatly cut into the Beaux Arts façade, can make AKA easy to miss, but do check out this discreet hotel, opened in 2007. The 81 suites were carved out of a 1920s apartment block and each has a fully equipped kitchen, echoing the building's residential roots. The décor is modern, with darkwood furnishings, oversized leather headboards and architecturally themed artwork. The Penthouse Suites offer up to 120 sq m of space, and the best rooms are on the hotel's south-west corner, with a view over Rittenhouse Square. This isn't a full-service hotel (there's no pool or restaurant), but guests have access to the Philadelphia Sports Club and staff will do their best to accommodate every request. *135 S 18th Street, T 215 825 7000, hotelaka.com*

Loews
This hotel is housed in the 1932 PSFS
Building (see p066), one of America's
finest modernist skyscrapers. A $115m
overhaul in 2000 converted the former
offices into 603 rooms and suites,
furnished by Daroff Design. Rooms
such as the Luxury King (pictured) on
the 28th floor offer great skyline views.
*1200 Market Street, T 215 627 1200,
www.loewshotels.com/philadelphia*

24 HOURS

SEE THE BEST OF THE CITY IN JUST ONE DAY

Most visitors to Philly make a beeline for Independence Mall to see the greatest hits of colonial America. There's nothing wrong with that, but we would like to show you the city's other side: its dynamic creative scene, fine neighbourhood eateries and bars, and modern architecture. The centre is compact enough to explore on foot, while in University City you could do like a local and hire some wheels at Trophy Bikes (3131 Walnut Street, T 215 222 2020).

For breakfast, try Fork:etc (opposite) in Old City, a great spot for eating in or grabbing something to go. The surrounding area is full of independent shops and galleries, and Art in the Age of Mechanical Reproduction (see p026) is among the best. North of here is the edgier but on-the-up neighbourhood Northern Liberties – a magnet for local artists and worth exploring. Next, head across town to University City, for a bite at White Dog Cafe (see p037) and a visit to the Institute of Contemporary Art (see p028). Architourists may want to venture further into the University of Pennsylvania campus to see Frank Furness' 1891 Fisher Fine Arts Library (220 S 34th Street, T 215 898 8325).

As you wind down your day, we suggest drinks with a view at XIX (see p050), followed by dinner at Mercato (see p030) in Washington Square West. Afterwards, you're steps from the nightlife of Rittenhouse or a nightcap at APO Bar + Lounge (see p031). *For full addresses, see Resources.*

09.30 Fork:etc

Ellen Yin opened Fork:etc, the casual arm of her hugely successful restaurant Fork (T 215 625 9425), in 2004 to capitalise on Old City's burgeoning population – and it's turned out to be the type of place that every 'hood should have. Local designer Marguerite Rodgers created the small space next door to the restaurant, adding dark wood, a communal table and a large window overlooking Market Street.

The vibe is easygoing and the food is tasty breakfast fare, fresh breads and pâtisserie, with the emphasis on takeaway orders; they make a great grilled ham, egg and cheese sandwich. Order this to go with a cup of the locally roasted coffee, La Colombe, and you've got a portable meal perfect for a walkabout.
*308 Market Street, T 215 625 9425,
forkrestaurant.com/forketc.htm*

11.00 Art in the Age

Artist-designed T-shirts can be two a penny these days, but don't leave town without picking up one from Art in the Age of Mechanical Reproduction (the name is taken from the 1936 essay by Walter Benjamin). Steven Grasse launched the brand in 2006 with a range of hand-sewn, custom-dyed designs. Two years later, he opened this store, filling it with an eclectic selection of local products (quilts, artwork, stationery, Art in the Age's own root beer, see p073), and clothing lines you won't find elsewhere in the city. Philadelphia-based architects Rissay created the space, installing a mix of modern and reclaimed furniture, including a 1940s apothecary cabinet. *116 N 3rd Street, T 215 922 2600, artintheage.com*

14.30 Institute of Contemporary Art

Pay attention to the work displayed at Philly's ICA. Since it was founded in 1963, the museum has had a knack for catching artists on their way up. It featured Agnes Martin, Cy Twombly, Robert Mapplethorpe and Andy Warhol, among others, before they became art superstars. The museum itself, housed in a 1991 building designed by Adèle Naudé Santos, mounts exhibitions in all media and hosts events including the Whenever Wednesday series, which can involve lectures, performance art, film screenings or workshops. There's a great museum shop here too – the only one on the East Coast to sell the full line of the fun artist multiples created by Philadelphia-based collective Cerealart (cerealart.com). *118 S 36th Street, T 215 898 7108, icaphila.org*

20.00 Mercato

Philadelphia does laid-back neighbourhood restaurants very well, and there's often a queue for a seat at this BYOB just off Avenue of the Arts. The corner, 35-cover dining room manages to be cosy rather than claustrophobic, thanks to the warm colour scheme and exposed brick – a nice change from the starkness of some of the city's other BYOBs (they are lots of these in Philly and there's usually a charge for corkage). Chef Mackenzie Hilton's menu marries seasonal classic and modern Italian cooking – the seafood and red meat dishes are especially good. If you want a non-alcoholic drink, try one of Mercato's Italian sodas, which are available by the glass or the pitcher. The restaurant accepts cash only.
1216 Spruce Street, T 215 985 2962, mercatobyob.com

22.30 APO Bar + Lounge

Spend a little time at APO and you'll see that everything is dedicated to bartending and mixology as artforms. The drinks, design of the space and the bar's name all take their inspiration from the apothecary — and the cocktails are a proper showcase of ingredients and flavours. The list covers original concoctions and twists on the classics, made with all manner of tinctures and extracts, fresh juices and syrups, and lesser known spirits. Brothers Sam and Tim Shaaban came up with APO's concept, and their design firm, Urban Space Development, created the two-level interior — a mix of black, green, white marble and oak — which includes a roof terrace. Closed Mondays and Tuesdays. *102 S 13th Street, T 215 735 7500, apothecarylounge.com*

URBAN LIFE
CAFÉS, RESTAURANTS, BARS AND NIGHTCLUBS

Eating out in Philadelphia is a wonderful thing. This is a city that takes its food seriously, whether you're talking greasy spoons like the venerable Mayfair Diner (7373 Frankford Avenue, T 215 624 4455), sophisticated restaurants such as James (see p041), or local speciality, the Philly cheesesteak sandwich. You'll get plenty of advice as to who serves the best, but many Philadelphians swear by Jim's Steaks (400 South Street, T 215 928 1911).

At the higher end, two chefs dominate: Stephen Starr, whose ever-expanding empire includes tongue-in-cheek American diner Jones (700 Chestnut Street, T 215 223 5663) and the steakhouse Barclay Prime (opposite); and Jose Garces, a Starr alum who made an impression with his tapas bar Amada (see p049) and Peruvian-Cantonese eaterie Chifa (707 Chestnut Street, T 215 925 5555). Another name to watch is Daniel Stern. His University City restaurant MidAtlantic (3711 Market Street, T 215 386 3711) focuses on historic Pennsylvanian flavours and ingredients.

Philadelphia's nightlife is not quite as slick. Too many clubs, especially in Rittenhouse, try to match those in New York; G (111 S 17th Street, T 215 564 1515) leads the pack, with its velvet rope and private Mogul Room. Far better are the places with less attitude and more atmosphere, like L'Etage (see p046) and the live music venue Johnny Brenda's (1201 N Frankford Avenue, T 215 739 9684). *For full addresses, see Resources.*

Barclay Prime

There is a glut of high-profile steakhouses in the city right now, each with its own gimmick. Stephen Starr's Barclay Prime has its share of flashiness (it did, after all, once advertise a $100 Kobe cheesesteak), but look past that and you'll see Barclay for what it is – a seriously good restaurant. The ribeye, from New York butcher Gachot & Gachot, is excellent, and the house tater tots (fried nuggets of grated potato) have a well-deserved cult following. Paris-based India Mahdavi brought her signature style to the venue, designing the interiors around the original features of the space – the ground floor of the 1929 Barclay Building, formerly a hotel. The result is clubby but modern, with a wood-panelled bar/lounge and large dining room (above).
237 S 18th Street, T 215 732 7560, barclayprime.com

Supper

Somewhere between a Philly BYOB and an upscale Rittenhouse eaterie, Supper serves tapas-sized plates of new American cuisine. Chef Mitch Prensky co-owns the venue with his wife, Jennifer, and while the food is squarely in the fine-dining camp, the room itself is all about low-key comfort.

926 South Street, T 215 592 8180, supperphilly.com

Capogiro Gelato Artisans

Stephanie Reitano got hooked on *gelato* when she had her first taste in 2001. The following year, she and her Italian-born husband, John, imported equipment from Italy, and Capogiro was born. Architect John Wagner designed this, the company's first venue, with custom-designed lighting fixtures modelled after ones Stephanie had seen in a bar in Milan. But the star here is the ice cream, all made daily in Philly using local ingredients (the milk and much of the fruit comes from nearby Lancaster County). The 27 flavours distributed to the four Philly Capogiros may include lime-coriander, pomegranate, burnt sugar and *stracciatella*. It'll take you a while to work through them all, but we can't think of a more delicious project.
119 S 13th Street, T 215 351 0900, capogirogelato.com

White Dog Cafe

Twenty-five years ago Judy Wicks opened a coffee and muffin shop in a University City brownstone. Since then, White Dog Cafe has evolved into a restaurant and a Philadelphia institution. Chef Eric Yost's contemporary American menu runs from salads and sandwiches to pasta and seafood dishes (the weekend brunch of homemade waffles and omelettes is worth coming back for if you miss it on your first visit). The drinks list features lots of American labels and includes Leg Lifter Lager, the house beer. But there's more to White Dog than the menu; the café gives back by promoting minority-owned sister restaurants, mentoring local students and hosting community storytelling sessions.

3420 Sansom Street, T 215 386 9224, whitedog.com

Grocery

Given Center City's urbanity, there's a
surprising lack of decent takeout options.
Until the competition arrives, head
to Valerie Safran and Marcie Turney's
corner market, opened in 2006. Many of
the recipes are Turney's, who was a 2009
James Beard Award nominee for her
work at Bindi (T 215 922 6061) next door.
*101 S 13th Street, T 215 922 5252,
grocery13.com/grocery13*

Osteria

Seats at Marc Vetri's eponymous Spruce
Street restaurant (T 215 732 3478) are
among the most sought after in the city,
but his more casual venue, Osteria, has
been turning heads too. Opened in 2007
in a former warehouse, this airy, industrial
space with a red-stained concrete floor
is a spot-on setting for Vetri's rustic Italian
food. Osteria's pizza has earned the lion's
share of the attention, and the Lombarda,
with baked egg, *Bitto* cheese, mozzarella
and *cotechino* sausage on a super-thin
crust, is definitely a hit and makes a great
lunch if time is tight. The wine list has 100
or so Italian bottles to choose from, and
the desserts are as good as the savoury
dishes. Try the moreish *polenta budino*,
topped with *gianduia* and candied nuts.
*640 N Broad Street, T 215 763 0920,
osteriaphilly.com*

James

Husband-and-wife team Kristina and Jim Burke (she's the manager, he's the chef) run one of the city's don't-miss restaurants on a quiet South Philly street not too far from the Italian Market. Burke, a former member of Marc Vetri's kitchen (opposite), built his modern Italian-American menu around seasonal local produce, meat and seafood. Expect richly flavoured dishes like tagliatelle with duck ragu, shaved chocolate and orange, and a slow-roasted poularde with an apple-scented sauce that has become a signature dish. The décor in the dining room is clean-lined and unfussy, and the adjacent lounge is a great place for a cocktail. The tasting menu (served for dinner only, Tuesday to Thursday) has received rave reviews.

824 S 8th Street, T 215 629 4980, jameson8th.com

Union Trust

This Center City restaurant may have rivals for the title of best steakhouse in town, but it does win our vote for most stunning location. The Victorian building was originally built to house three banks, then remodelled in 1923 by local architect Paul Philippe Cret. In 2009, Philadelphia firm DAS converted the banking hall into the epitome of US power dining – at a cost of a cool $12m. The renovation preserved the gilded 20m-high ceiling and travertine walls and added a mezzanine level, expanding the seating to 300. The steak is as serious as the décor. Most of it comes from Chicago butcher Allen Brothers and is available in the standard cuts, including long bone dry-aged ribeyes. Charcuterie, a raw bar and a seafood menu are also available, plus some 18,000 bottles of wine.
717 Chestnut Street, T 215 925 6000, uniontruststeakhouse.com

Pub & Kitchen

The name says it all. This 2008 eaterie just off Rittenhouse Square is a friendly neighbourhood pub with an exceptional kitchen – no more and no less. Owners Dan Clark and Ed Hackett converted a corner building at the end of a row of houses, installing a long 1940s-era bar and a small dining area (above), where church pews serve as banquettes. Head chef Jonathan McDonald handles the food, which is equally uncluttered. His take on fish and chips (beer-battered hake or pollock with a side of buttery mushy peas) is as good as you'll find anywhere, and his Windsor Burger, with English cheddar, Bibb lettuce, tomato and pork-belly strips on brioche is another hit. The beer list is also draw for P&K's loyal local clientele.
1946 Lombard Street, T 215 545 0350, thepubandkitchen.com

Vintage

Delphine and Jason Evenchik have created a little gem here – the wine bar/bistro they opened in Midtown Village in 2006. The drinks list offers enough surprises to keep oenophiles interested, but prices are affordable for the 80 or so wines that Delphine hand-picks from the new and old worlds. Smaller vineyards in the western US, South America, Africa and Europe are represented, and the tasting notes (or knowledgeable staff) will help you navigate the list. The décor is sparse but cosy, thanks to the wooden floors and brick walls, with a centrepiece wrought-iron sculpture by local artist Vin Marshall. Vintage also offers a selection of artisanal beers (mostly European) and a short menu of dishes like bruschetta and burgers.
129 S 13th Street, T 215 922 3095, vintage-philadelphia.com

L'Etage

The owners of this South Philly bar already had a hit with their crêperie, Beau Monde, so when they decided to open a lounge in 2003 it made sense to locate it above the eaterie. Jim Caiola and David Salama's L'Etage quickly became one of the city's best nightspots. The furnishings – leather seating, Fortuny wall coverings and velvet drapery tinted by local textile artist Kevin O'Brien – were well chosen for the smallish space, which oozes atmosphere compared with some of the city's other nightlife venues. Regular entertainment is provided by DJs, but things really heat up on cabaret nights, when the acts range from jazz to burlesque. Snag an ottoman, lie back and enjoy. If you're peckish, there are menus for crêpes and bar food.
624 S 6th Street, T 215 592 0656, creperie-beaumonde.com

Continental Mid-town

The original Old City branch of Stephen Starr's Continental (T 215 923 6069) has its charm, but for showmanship it can't hold a candle to the venue Starr opened near Rittenhouse Square in 2004. Stokes Architecture and Shawn Hausman Design conceived the interior, which has a witty edge with its vinyl booths, hanging wicker chairs, tiled walls and shag carpeting on the ceiling. The global menu is similarly playful. Try the surprisingly addictive cheesesteak eggrolls served with *sriracha* ketchup, with The Astronaut, a cocktail made from peach vodka, triple sec and Tang. Continental Mid-town is garish but oddly appealing, which likely accounts for the hip crowd that packs the three-level space at weekends.
1801 Chestnut Street, T 215 567 1800, continentalmidtown.com

Amada

Jose Garces introduced Philadelphia to tapas when he opened this eaterie in 2005, and today, even with dozens of competitors, the restaurant remains at the top of the small-plate heap. Though the menu sticks close to the classics, the presentation is fresh and modern; drinks include several variations on sangria, Emilio Hildalgo sherries and a strong Spanish wine list. The interior, designed by Jun Aizaki of Brooklyn-based firm Crème Design, features an open kitchen that gives onto the bar (above) and a handsome dining room fitted with black wood cabinetry and reclaimed-lumber furnishings. If you can't get a reservation here, try Garces' other tapas bar, Tinto (T 215 665 9150), in Rittenhouse Square. *217-219 Chestnut Street, T 215 625 2450, amadarestaurant.com*

XIX

The Bellevue-Stratford Hotel was the city's last word in luxury when it opened its doors in 1904: the 'grande dame of Broad Street', as locals called it. Though the hotel of that era is long gone, you can still see flashes of its elegance in the restaurant/bar XIX, on the 19th storey of what is now a Park Hyatt. Interior designer Marguerite Rodgers enhanced original details such as the pilasters and high-domed ceiling. The bar (above), which is located between the two dining rooms, offers one of the best views of the Philly skyline you'll find. Despite the formal surroundings, XIX is casual enough for a cocktail if you're dropping in off the street. *200 S Broad Street, T 215 790 1919, nineteenrestaurant.com*

Noble

Tucked down an unassuming block in Rittenhouse Square, Noble bills itself as an 'American cookery'. And that's precisely what it delivers, with aplomb. Dishes on chef Steven Duane Cameron's menu are built around the numerous influences in American cuisine, but all are centred on top-quality ingredients and pared-down preparations. Expect simple grilled or roasted meat and fish, vegetables from the restaurant's own rooftop garden, and excellent breads and pâtisserie made in-house. American wines and beers drive Noble's concept home. Upstairs, the airy dining room (above) captures the feel of an urban farmhouse, while on the ground floor, outside seating (in summer) faces into a lounge/bar area. *2025 Sansom Street, T 215 568 7000, noblecookery.com*

Distrito

Jose Garces' Mexican restaurant in University City is huge fun. The two-level space, designed by Jun Aizaki (his Amada collaborator; see p049), features a wall of around 600 Mexican wrestling masks along the staircase and a booth made from the shell of a VW Beetle. Luckily, there's substance behind the style in the form of chef Tim Spinner's cheeky but refined take on Mexico City cuisine (the tuna ceviche is made with a serrano-coconut sauce and lime sorbet; the grilled meats are brushed with pineapple and grapefruit), and the fact that it's all plated beautifully. Things tend to get raucous, especially when the nearby universities are in term time, but after a few fresh-fruit margaritas you really won't mind. *3945 Chestnut Street, T 215 222 1657, distritorestaurant.com*

INSIDER'S GUIDE

MELANIE STEPANIK, RETAIL BUYER

Originally from Ohio, Melanie Stepanik has lived in Philly since 2003. She lives and works, as buyer for Art in the Age of Mechanical Reproduction (see po26), in Old City, which she admires for its laid-back feel, friendly residents and shops lining N 2nd and 3rd Streets. Her standout stores are Reward (55 N 2nd Street, T 267 773 8675), which sells fashion exclusive to the city or the US, and, just south of the neighbourhood, Anastacia's Antiques (617 Bainbridge Street, T 215 928 9111). 'It's hard to walk out of there without picking up something,' she confesses. Another regular stop is the art collective shop/gallery Space 1026 (see po82).

Distrito (see po52) and Bar Ferdinand (1030 N 2nd Street, T 215 923 1313) in Northern Liberties are two of Stepanik's haunts for drinks and a bite to eat, or if she's in Rittenhouse Square, Snackbar (253 S 20th Street, T 215 545 5655). For a caffeine hit, she heads to La Colombe Torrefaction (130 S 19th Street, T 215 563 0860) and for something sweet it's ice cream at the retro-style Franklin Fountain (116 Market Street, T 215 627 1899). Later on, she'll meet friends at Silk City (435 Spring Garden Street, T 215 592 8838) or Johnny Brenda's (1201 N Frankford Avenue, T 215 739 9684).

When the city gets too much, she drives out of town for a game of tennis or a hike in the beautiful wooded Wissahickon Valley, which is part of Fairmount Park (T 215 683 0200).

For full addresses, see Resources.

ARCHITOUR

A GUIDE TO PHILADELPHIA'S ICONIC BUILDINGS

From the redbrick austerity of colonialism to the glassy bravado of contemporary commerce, much of the entire history of American architecture is on display in Philadelphia. Though many leading 19th-century architects were trained here, the cityscape remained traditional for years, punctuated by flashes of brilliance such as Frank Furness and George Hewitt's 1876 Pennsylvania Academy of the Fine Arts (118 N Broad Street, T 215 972 7600), the 1932 PSFS Building (see p066), designed by George Howe and William Lescaze, and Frank Lloyd Wright's often overlooked 1959 Beth Sholom Synagogue (8231 Old York Road, T 215 887 1342).

Innovation in local architecture began in earnest in the 1960s. Led by a group of architects and planners including Robert Venturi, Denise Scott Brown, Ian McHarg and Louis Kahn, the Philadelphia School moved past the modernist glass box into contextualism; structures such as Kahn's Richards Medical Research Building (see p062) at the University of Pennsylvania, Robert Geddes' 1963 Police Headquarters (see p067) and Venturi's postmodern 1964 Vanna Venturi House, a private residence for his mother, paved the way for new architecture nationwide. Today, the city is full of energy once again and working to refine itself through new landmarks in the mould of César Pelli's Cira Centre (opposite) and quietly impressive buildings such as Skirkanich Hall (see p068). *For full addresses, see Resources.*

Cira Centre

If developers have their way, the 2005 Cira Centre will eventually be just one of many skyscrapers on the west bank of the Schuylkill. But for now, it draws much of its impact from the fact that it stands alone. César Pelli gave the 133m building a faceted profile and covered it in cool blue glass that gleams like quartz crystal in certain light and creates a dramatic counterpoint to the stone 30th Street Station (see p064) across the road. At night, a grid of colour-changing LEDs integrated into the curtain wall accents the tower's distinctive profile. The location that helps make the building so dramatic also means it lacks spark at street level (it's sandwiched between the station and railway tracks), but with luck development along 30th Street will help change that. *2929 Arch Street, ciracentre.com*

Kimmel Center
It's hard to know what to think about the
$235m Kimmel Center, opened in 2001 as
the home of the Philadelphia Orchestra.
Architect Rafael Viñoly's 45m-high glass
barrel vault created an interior plaza
which he intended to be a major civic
space, but at times can seem more like
an empty shopping mall. The mahogany-
lined Verizon Hall is wonderful, though.
260 S Broad Street, T 215 670 2327

Society Hill Towers

This group of three residential towers, completed in 1963 on the site of a food market, was the zenith of a massive rehabilitation of Society Hill, one of the city's oldest areas. IM Pei designed the complex with his customary attention to detail: the buildings are positioned so that none blocks the others' views, their carefully articulated concrete-and-glass façades reflecting both the geometry of the surrounding streets and the Federal and Georgian terraces that line them. The result remains a highly sought-after address nearly 50 years on. If you don't secure an invitation to one of the private residences, you can still appreciate the towers from the motor court, which features Leonard Baskin's sculptural set *Old Man, Young Man, The Future.*
S 2nd Street/Locust Street

WCAU Building

A 1920s construction boom left Philly with some fine art deco architecture, though little of it is quite as flamboyant as this 1928 building designed for radio station WCAU. Architects Gabriel Roth and Harry Sternfeld studded the façade with reflective cobalt glass chips, surrounded the windows with zigzag panels made of brass, copper and stainless steel and topped the structure with a glazed, illuminated tower bearing the station's letters (the tower was later removed, but the WCAU lettering remains on the lift doors inside). Numerous renovations over the years have left little of the original interiors intact, though the building's current occupier, the Art Institute of Philadelphia, carried out an exterior restoration in the early 1990s.
1622 Chestnut Street

Richards Medical Research Building
When the University of Pennsylvania
commissioned Louis Kahn to design a
high-rise laboratory in 1957, the architect
had no experience working with high-rises
or labs. But Kahn met the challenge – and
influenced modern architecture – by
dividing the complex, which includes the
Goddard Laboratories, into its functional
components: the 'servant' and 'served',
as he called them. Completed in 1965, five
lab and classroom towers are grouped
around two core buildings containing
mechanical and support systems; inside
the lab towers, Kahn created open-plan,
column-free spaces made possible by
engineer August Komendant's pre-stressed
concrete structural system. Occupants
have since subdivided the open laboratories
and blocked the expanses of plate glass,
as the design turned out not to be as
practical as Kahn had hoped.
3700-3800 Hamilton Walk

30th Street Station
Chicago architects Graham, Anderson, Probst & White made the most of this station's site, pointing its neoclassical columned portico towards the central skyline on the other bank of the Schuylkill. The massive proportions of the building, opened in 1933, are reflected in the stunning main concourse (pictured), lit by five-storey windows and deco chandeliers.
N 30th Street/Market Street

PSFS Building

It seems odd that America's oldest savings bank would have built the world's most modern skyscraper as its headquarters, but the Philadelphia Savings Fund Society did just that. Some 80 years on, this International Style building looks as fresh as when it opened in 1932. Local architect George Howe and his Swiss partner, William Lescaze, designed the 150m tower with sleek, modern lines and materials including granite and marble imported from 32 countries; the building cost $8m, an almost unimaginable figure in the Depression. Architects Bower Lewis Thrower converted the office space into guest rooms and carried out a restoration of the public areas for the opening of the Loews hotel (see p022) in 2000.
12 S 12th Street

Philadelphia Police Headquarters

The Roundhouse, as locals call this police headquarters, doesn't always get the love it deserves. Philadelphians associate the building with past police scandals, and officials complain that it is ill-suited to the needs of a modern force. That's a shame, because there's a lot to like in architect Robert Geddes' design. Geddes anchored the building, which was completed in 1963, with twin drum-shaped towers and wrapped it in a precast concrete skin. The result – a measured modernist structure with a sinuous form – is a blend of strength and grace, although the blank wall surrounding it doesn't do it any favours. The police are talking about relocating to a more traditional building, a move that may allow the Roundhouse to be seen with fresh eyes.
1 Franklin Square

Skirkanich Hall

Rather than deferring to the traditional red brick architecture of the rest of the campus, New York's Tod Williams Billie Tsien Architects faced the University of Pennsylvania's new bioengineering building, opened in 2006, in shingled glass, aluminium, zinc and glazed brick in a range of shades from black to chartreuse. The combination is at once high-tech and organic, and blends beautifully with both the early 20th-century buildings nearby and with KieranTimberlake's glassy Levine Hall to the west. Do walk through Skirkanich's atrium, where cherrywood and glazed blue and yellow tiles accent the black granite finishes and exposed-concrete structure, which has been polished, hammered and sandblasted to suggest handworked stone.
210 S 33rd Street

Perelman Building
The first phase of the expansion plan for the Philadelphia Museum of Art (see p014) set a high standard for what is to come. Gluckman Mayner Architects reworked the 1927 Fidelity Mutual Life Insurance Company Building, preserving its art deco façade and monumental entrances while creating six galleries, conservation space and a library inside. *2525 Pennsylvania Avenue*

SHOPPING

THE BEST RETAIL THERAPY AND WHAT TO BUY

Unfortunately for Philadelphia, New York casts a long retail shadow, and local shops often lose out on the attention they should attract because all eyes are focused north. But there's a lot to like here in Philly and a host of innovative retailers to discover.

Center City's two main shopping destinations couldn't be more different. Around lower Market Street, N 2nd Street and N 3rd Street, you'll find a clutch of hip clothiers such as Sugarcube (see p086) and Topstitch (54 N 3rd Street, T 215 238 8877), as well as megastore Foster's Homeware (33 N 3rd Street, T 215 925 0950). Across town, in Rittenhouse Square, independent shops including Joan Shepp (1616 Walnut Street, T 215 735 2666) hold their own among the big names along Walnut Street, while Joseph Fox Bookshop (1724 Sansom Street, T 215 563 4184) has been serving the local literati for around 60 years.

Upcoming areas to watch include Midtown Village and the compact strip of stores on the section of S 13th Street near Walnut; located here are the boutique Modern Eye (145 S 13th Street, T 215 922 3300), which sells a collection of limited-edition eyewear, and the savonnier Duross & Langel (117 S 13th Street, T 215 592 7627). To the south, ventures such as the smart home accessories shop Jimmy Style (1820 E Passyunk Avenue, T 267 239 0598) are leading the charge in Passyunk Square, one of the city's current hot spots. *For full addresses, see Resources.*

Root beer

Among the eclectic list of items invented in Philadelphia (the revolving door, bubblegum, bifocals and rolled toilet paper), root beer – a drink that dates back to colonial times – remains relatively unknown beyond North America. It was first marketed by local pharmacist Charles Hires in 1876, whose original (non-alcoholic) formula included sarsaparilla, sassafras, wild cherry and ginger, though today you'll come across numerous variations around the country. To honour Philly's connection with the drink, Art in the Age of Mechanical Reproduction (see p026) came up with Root ($32.99 for 720ml), a heady alcoholic version based on an early recipe. Try it with ginger ale or check out the suggestions on the website. Available at local liquor stores and bars. *artintheage.com/spirits-aita*

Bahdeebahdu

Named after a dog who lived in Old City (you'll get the whole story when you call in), Bahdeebahdu is located in a former garage building in Kensington South, which is well off the usual shopping track. The studio/gallery space is a partnership between interior designer RJ Thornburg and artist Warren Muller, who creates his light sculptures and chandeliers on site from found or recycled objects like car parts, musical instruments and cutlery. There's also a selection of furniture and art by local designers, including the collective MONA. Prices are high (Muller's work ranges from about $1,000 to around $25,000), but even if you aren't buying, Bahdeebahdu is worth the trip to get the inside track on the local design scene.

1522 N American Street, T 215 627 5002, bahdeebahdu.com

AKA Music

True, you can get almost any musical recording you want on the internet these days, but there's something deeply satisfying about riffling through the racks of an independent bricks-and-mortar music store – especially if it's as good as Old Town's AKA. The long, narrow store is a fairly spartan space, with a mezzanine level where local bands occasionally perform, and bin upon bin of new and used CDs, DVDs and vinyl. The rigorous genre divisions, from Japanese psychedelic rock to 1960s soul/garage, should help you in your search, although the filing system breaks down somewhat in the used section. More often than not, a little patience will yield something wonderful, and the helpful staff are always willing to make recommendations.

27 N 2nd Street, T 215 922 3855

AIA Bookstore & Design Center

Fittingly for a city with such a rich architectural heritage, its best design bookstore is run by the local chapter of the American Institute of Architects. Stocked with a tightly edited range of titles, the shop has been running since 1976; it moved to its current location, on the ground floor of a century-old former factory, in 2008. The section on local buildings and history is excellent, and its range of smart stationery and home accessories has proved a hit with locals. As a bonus, the Center for Architecture (T 215 569 3186) is in the same building, and offers a programme of lectures, exhibitions and guided tours if you want to learn more about Philadelphia's built environment.

1218 Arch Street, T 215 569 3188, aiabookstore.com

Billykirk

Brothers Chris and Kirk Bray got into the leather business almost by accident, inspired by a 1970s watchstrap Kirk found in a pawn shop (the pair are avid vintage shoppers). When they decided to take up leatherwork full time, they went all in, studying under a master craftsman in LA. The result was Billykirk – a line of belts, bags, wallets and accessories founded in 1999 and inspired by classic, functional designs. All the products are handmade in the US, with the majority of the leatherwork entrusted to Amish craftsmen in Pennsylvania's Lancaster County. We were rather taken with this waxed-cotton carryall, $320 (above), and the brand's signature handstitched luggage tag. Art in the Age of Mechanical Reproduction (see p026) is a stockist, or visit the website. *billykirk.com*

Ubiq
Even non-trainerheads should pay
a visit to Ubiq. Housed in a converted
townhouse, the store stocks covetable
lines from the big brands, plus its own
range of footwear and an array of
hip streetwear. It's all showcased in
snazzy digs by New York-based Rafael
de Cárdenas of Architecture at Large.
*1509 Walnut Street, T 215 988 0194,
ubiqlife.com*

Store 1026

Local artist collective Space 1026 has been producing edgy work out of its walk-up studios and gallery since it was founded in 1997. It wasn't until 2008, though, that the group's focus on affordable art led to a shop. In truth, the store is really just a section of the high-ceilinged gallery (right), but it does stock a good range of handmade prints, books, films, T-shirts and 'zines, as well as works from current and past exhibitions. Best of all, most items are priced well under $50. Retail traffic usually centres on show openings, but pieces are available online and you're always free to wander in and see what's going on in the gallery (ring the bell downstairs for entry). Look out for 1026's annual art auction in December.

1026 Arch Street, T 215 574 7630, store1026.com

Josh Owen
Philadelphia-based industrial designer
Josh Owen has created work for Areaware,
Casamania, Kikkerland and Umbra,
and his pieces are regularly featured in
exhibitions worldwide. He has also shown
at the Salone Internazionale del Mobile
in Milan. One of the reasons his work is
so well regarded is its multifunctionalism:
his 'SOS' stool (right), for example, can
be used as a serving tray, with the side
projections doubling as handles and
holders for cups or wine glasses; turned
upside down, it becomes a large vase.
Both the Centre Pompidou in Paris and
the Philadelphia Museum of Art (see p014)
added the 'SOS' to their permanent
collections in 2008. You can view and
buy Owen's work at Foster's Homeware
(see p072) or at his South Philly studio
(call ahead to make an appointment).
700 S 10th Street, T 215 923 4856,
joshowen.com

Sugarcube
Elisa Buratto has a talent for finding choice vintage pieces, and her Old City boutique is known, in particular, for its cocktail dresses, spectacle frames, jewellery and cowboy boots. But not everything here is vintage; Sugarcube also carries men's and women's clothing from the likes of APC and Steven Alan.
124 N 3rd Street, T 215 238 0825, sugarcube.us

SPORTS AND SPAS
WORK OUT, CHILL OUT OR JUST WATCH

Sport is a religion for many Philadelphians. If you need proof, head out on S Broad Street to the stadiums where the city's professional teams for basketball (76ers), ice hockey (Flyers), baseball (Phillies) and American football (Eagles) play. No matter how badly the teams are doing (and they often are), lively local fans will be there in force. And in US sports history, few venues are quite as storied as The Palestra (overleaf), the University of Pennsylvania's basketball arena. Go along to see what a game is like without all the flashy modern trappings. For a workout of your own, there's the Fairmount Park System (fairmountpark.org). At 3,725 hectares, it's the largest municipal park in the country, and a great place to go hiking, cycling, rowing or horseriding. The largest area, Fairmount Park itself (Avenue of the Republic, T 215 683 0200), is easily accessible from any location in Center City.

Philadelphia's spa culture is certainly not as developed as New York's, but there are several top-quality pampering palaces to be found. For boys, the barbershop Groom (opposite) offers a classic, old-fashioned wet shave, while girls can get a brush up at Laurentius Salon (815 Christian Street, T 215 238 0764), housed in a striking three-storey glass building in South Philly's Italian Market neighbourhood. For men and women, we suggest the small but super-efficient Rescue Rittenhouse Spa (see p092).

For full addresses, see Resources.

Groom

Owner Joe McMenamin has created a gem of a barbershop here in downtown Philly. Trained by a barber who had been in business since the 1930s, McMenamin opened his own venue, Groom, in 2005, relocating to this basement space in Washington Square West in 2008. Lined with white subway tiles and dark wood, it's an atmospheric and distinctly old-school setting for a haircut and straight-razor shave, with hot and cold towels, and McMenamin's own astringent (one of his few concessions to fashion). Expect plenty of barber banter and an expert shave while you listen to the owner's impeccable jazz collection. Make sure you call ahead, as walk-ins can't be guaranteed an appointment. *1324 Locust Street, T 215 545 2626, groomphilly.com*

The Palestra

'To win the game is great. To play the game is greater. But to love the game is the greatest of all,' says a plaque inside The Palestra. And for those who love college basketball, there are few places more important than this. Since 1927, the court has hosted more college games than any other facility in the US. Architect Charles Klauder designed the building and it was named by the university's professor of Greek, William N Bates. The barrel roof is supported by 10 steel trusses, which give the venue its famous open sightlines. Come to see a game (the season runs from mid-October to March) and you won't find any VIP boxes or electronic scoreboards, but you'll understand why The Palestra is dubbed the Cathedral of College Basketball. *220 S 32nd Street, T 215 898 6151, pennathletics.com*

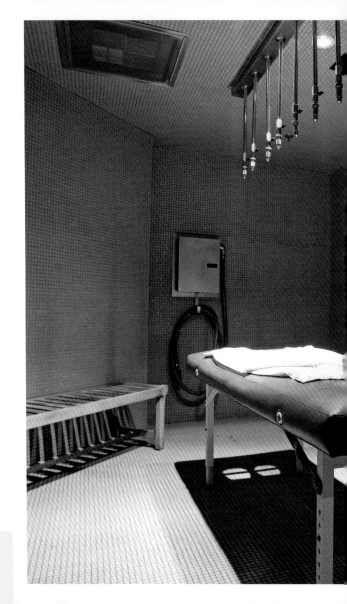

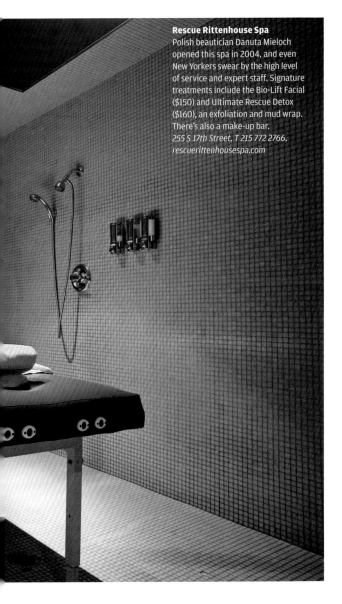

Rescue Rittenhouse Spa
Polish beautician Danuta Mieloch
opened this spa in 2004, and even
New Yorkers swear by the high level
of service and expert staff. Signature
treatments include the Bio-Lift Facial
($150) and Ultimate Rescue Detox
($160), an exfoliation and mud wrap.
There's also a make-up bar.
255 S 17th Street, T 215 772 2766,
rescuerittenhousespa.com

North Bowl

This retro-style bowling alley is the result of owner Oron Daskal's quest to find a cool place for him and his friends to hang out. He didn't want to open a club or a bar, so he carved a bowling alley out of a former garage in Northern Liberties. The sprawling venue, which opened in 2006, has 17 lanes, two bars, an upstairs lounge, pool tables and an arcade, and at the weekend it gets packed to the rafters with a diverse crowd, from Northern Liberties hipsters to serious league bowlers. The globe lights and abundance of orange give the place a 1970s feel, but the bar areas are decidedly modern industrial. Snag a seat in the glass-enclosed lounge for a bird's-eye view of the bowling action and a taste of North Bowl's take on classic bowling-alley cuisine (corn dogs, burgers and numerous variations on tater tots).
909 N 2nd Street, T 215 238 2695, northbowlphilly.com

ESCAPES

WHERE TO GO IF YOU WANT TO LEAVE TOWN

Ask Philadelphians what they like best about their city, and one of the top answers will be how easy it is to leave. It isn't that locals are frantic to escape, but when they do, many of the best destinations in the north-east are within easy reach. Immediately to the west is Lancaster County, the home of the Pennsylvania Dutch (or Amish) community – a place that's full of both rural charm and touristy schmaltz. Stop in the city of Lancaster to eat at Central Market (23 N Market Street, T 717 735 6890; open Tuesdays, Fridays and Saturdays), the oldest farmers' market in the US; if you want to stay the night, try the Lancaster Arts Hotel (300 Harrisburg Avenue, T 717 299 3000). Further to the west is Pittsburgh, a city finding its post-industrial feet in its emerging neighbourhoods and cultural attractions, such as the Andy Warhol Museum (see p100). Nearby, take advantage of a rare chance to rent out a Frank Lloyd Wright property, the 1957 Duncan House (187 Evergreen Lane, Acme, T 877 833 7829; tours on Sunday).

And then there are two very traditional getaways still popular with Philadelphians: the New Jersey shore to the south-east and the Pocono mountains to the north; the best hotels are the retro-cool Chelsea in Atlantic City (opposite) and the historic Fauchère in Milford (see p102) respectively. If you're travelling north, stop off en route at the George Nakashima Studio Compound (overleaf). *For full addresses, see Resources.*

The Chelsea, Atlantic City

Set on the New Jersey shore, 100km from Philadelphia, Atlantic City once billed itself as the 'Queen of Resorts'. Then came postwar blight, then gambling, which did little to revive the city's fortunes – but if The Chelsea is any indication, things are looking up. Hotelier Curtis Bashaw opened the 332-room hotel in 2008, building on an existing 1965 Howard Johnson property. The interiors, designed by Bashaw's sister Colleen, have a midcentury feel, with plaid swivel chairs, mismatched lamps and muted tones (book the top-floor Rockstar Suite for its floor-to-ceiling windows and ocean views). The Chelsea doesn't have a casino, but its bars and lounges, and two restaurants run by Stephen Starr, are hip places to wine/dine and hang out. *111 S Chelsea Avenue, T 1 800 548 3030, thechelsea-ac.com*

George Nakashima complex
About an hour north of Philadelphia is New Hope, where Japanese-American architect and furniture craftsman George Nakashima settled in 1943. His former home and workshop complex, where his daughter Mira still produces work, was partly conceived by the designer. An experimental fusion of modernist and Japanese influences, it includes the 1957 Conoid Studio (pictured), whose arced concrete roof is just 6.35cm thick. The compound is open to the public on Saturday afternoons and consultations for commissions can be booked by appointment. The Moderne Gallery (111 N 3rd Street, T 215 923 8536) in Philadelphia also sells a selection of Nakashima's work. *1847 Aquetong Road, T 215 862 2272, nakashimawoodworker.com*

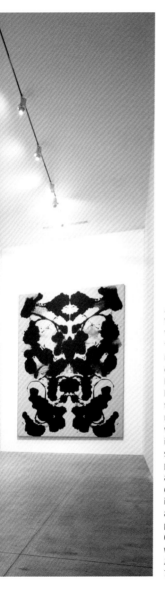

Andy Warhol Museum, Pittsburgh
When asked where he grew up, Andy Warhol would reply, 'I came from nowhere.' 'Nowhere' was Pittsburgh, a gritty steel manufacturing centre about 500km west of Philly, where the young Warhol spent his days studying movie magazines at home and the altar in church – experiences that would shape his consumerism-as-religion pop art. The Andy Warhol Museum, which opened in a former warehouse in 1994, holds thousands of his paintings, sculptures, drawings and photographs, plus an archive of his correspondence and diaries; it claims to be the most comprehensive single-artist collection in the world. Warhol's childhood home at 3252 Dawson Street (not open to the public) is a short drive from the excellent Carnegie Museum of Art (T 412 622 3131), where Warhol took art classes as a child.
117 Sandusky Street,
T 412 237 8300, warhol.org

Hotel Fauchère, Milford

When Swiss chef Louis Fauchère bought a hotel in picturesque Milford in 1867, he established both the town and the surrounding Poconos as a getaway for the well-to-do. But the Fauchère closed in 1976, and the pretty Italianate building was left to deteriorate. Fortunately, locals Sean Strub and Richard Snyder saw its potential, and reopened it in 2006 after a five-year restoration. New York-based designers Kureck Jones deftly combined a traditional look with modern touches, dressing the hotel in understated textiles and wallpaper; the 16 guest rooms are done out in beige and white, with Frette linens and heated Pennsylvania bluestone bathroom floors. Have dinner in the Delmonico Room, followed by a drink in chic Bar Louis. *401 Broad Street, T 570 409 1212, hotelfauchere.com*

NOTES
SKETCHES AND MEMOS

RESOURCES
CITY GUIDE DIRECTORY

HOTELS
ADDRESSES AND ROOM RATES

AKA Rittenhouse Square 021
Room rates:
studio, from $180
135 S 18th Street
T 215 825 7000
hotelaka.com

The Chelsea 097
Room rates:
double, from $139;
Rockstar Suite, from $3,000
111 S Chelsea Avenue
Atlantic City
T 1 800 548 3030
thechelsea-ac.com

Duncan House at Polymath Park Resort 096
Room rates:
House, from $425
187 Evergreen Lane
Acme
T 877 833 7829

Hotel Fauchère 102
Room rates:
double, from $200
401 Broad Street
Milford
T 570 409 1212
hotelfauchere.com

Four Seasons 016
Room rates:
double, from $395
1 Logan Square
T 215 963 1500
fourseasons.com/Philadelphia

Lancaster Arts Hotel 096
Room rates:
double, from $189
300 Harrisburg Avenue
Lancaster
T 717 299 3000
lancasterartshotel.com

Loews 022
Room rates:
double, from $179;
suite, from $500
Luxury King Room, from $199
1200 Market Street
T 215 627 1200
loewshotels.com/philadelphia

Le Méridien 016
Room rates:
prices on request
1421 Arch Street
T 215 422 8200
starwoodhotels.com/lemeridien

Hotel Palomar 018
Room rates:
double, from $152;
King Deluxe Room, from $229
117 S 17th Street
T 215 563 5006
hotelpalomar-philadelphia.com

The Rittenhouse 020
Room rates:
double, from $249;
suite, from $499
210 W Rittenhouse Square
T 215 546 9000
rittenhousehotel.com

The Ritz-Carlton 017
Room rates:
double, from $309;
suite, from $409;
Superior Room, from $429
10 S Broad Street
T 215 523 8000
ritzcarlton.com/philadelphia

WALLPAPER* CITY GUIDES

Editorial Director
Richard Cook

Art Director
Loran Stosskopf
Editor
Rachael Moloney
Author
Jim Parsons
Deputy Editor
Jeremy Case
Managing Editor
Jessica Diamond

Chief Designer
Daniel Shrimpton
Designer
Lara Collins

Map Illustrator
Russell Bell

Photography Editor
Sophie Corben
Photography Assistant
Robin Key

Sub-Editors
Vicky McGinlay
Stephen Patience
Editorial Assistant
Ella Marshall

Intern
Tiffany Jow

**Wallpaper* Group
Editor-in-Chief**
Tony Chambers
Publishing Director
Gord Ray

Contributors
Caroline Bean
Kevin Derrick
Jill Ivey
Beata Macos

Wallpaper* ® is a
registered trademark
of IPC Media Limited

First published 2010
© 2010 IPC Media Limited

ISBN 978 0 7148 5611 7

PHAIDON

Phaidon Press Limited
Regent's Wharf
All Saints Street
London N1 9PA

Phaidon Press Inc
180 Varick Street
New York, NY 10014

Phaidon® is a registered
trademark of Phaidon
Press Limited

www.phaidon.com

A CIP Catalogue record for
this book is available from
the British Library.

PHOTOGRAPHERS

Roger Casas
Philadelphia city view,
inside front cover
Independence Hall,
pp010-011
Comcast Center, p012
City Hall, p013
Philadelphia Museum
of Art, pp014-015
The Ritz-Carlton, p017
The Rittenhouse, p020
AKA Rittenhouse
Square, p021
Loews, pp022-023
Fork:etc, p025
Art in the Age of
Mechanical Reproduction,
pp026-027
Mercato, p030
APO Bar + Lounge, p031
Barclay Prime, p033
Supper, pp034-035
Capogiro Gelato
Artisans, p036
White Dog Cafe, p037
Grocery, pp038-039
Osteria, p040
James, p041
Union Trust, pp042-043
Pub & Kitchen, p044
Vintage, p045

Continental
Mid-town, p048
Amada, p049
XIX, p050
Noble, p051
Distrito, p052, p053
Melanie Stepanik, p055
Cira Centre, p057
Kimmel Center, pp058-059
Society Hill Towers, p060
WCAU Building, p061
Richards Medical Research
Building, pp062-063
30th Street Station,
pp064-065
PSFS Building, p066
Philadelphia Police
Headquarters, p067
Skirkanich Hall,
p068, p069
Perelman Building,
pp070-071
Bahdeebahdu, p074, p075
AKA Music, pp076-077
AIA Bookstore & Design
Center, p078
Ubiq, pp080-081
Sugarcube, pp086-087
Groom, p089
The Palestra, pp090-091
Rescue Rittenhouse Spa,
pp092-093
North Bowl, pp094-095

Peartree Digital
Root, p073

Esto
Conoid Studio, George
Nakashima complex,
pp098-099

Adam Wallacavage
Store 1026, pp082-083

PHILADELPHIA
A COLOUR-CODED GUIDE TO THE HOT 'HOODS

UNIVERSITY CITY
Situated west of the Schuylkill, the student heartland is noted for its vibrant nightlife

SOUTH PHILADELPHIA
Check out the cafés and shops catering to a diverse – Italian, Asian and Latino – population

FAIRMOUNT/ART MUSEUM
Tourists flock to the famous steps from *Rocky*, but seek out the spectacular river views

WASHINGTON SQUARE WEST
An intriguing mix of hipness and grit, Wash-West is catching up with the city's renewal

OLD CITY
Penn's waterfront stomping ground has cool shops and eateries amid the historic draws

CENTER CITY NORTH
Ignore the swarming suits; the business district also boasts markets and museums

RITTENHOUSE SQUARE
With upscale boutiques and the city's priciest properties, this is Philly at its most chichi

NORTHERN LIBERTIES
A prime example of recent gentrification, with ex-factories pulling in young bohemians

For a full description of each neighbourhood, see the Introduction.
Featured venues are colour-coded, according to the district in which they are located.